CONTENTS

I0505352

NOTE FROM THE AUTHOR

Thank you so much for taking time to read *A Month of...Service Advisor Tips.* This is just the beginning of a book series that will lead you to being a "better" service advisor or service manager.

As the Corporate Trainer for MOC Central, we want to offer you much more than an average vendor. We want to elevate our relationship to that of partner. Your success is ours and vice versa. The desire to be a partner with you drives us to push ourselves so we can help you become "better".

"Better" is in quotes because we feel that better means something different to everyone. If you are on a brand new job at a sparkling new facility, we can make you better. If you are an established veteran in a cutthroat market, we know we can make you better. MOC Central will work tirelessly to help you achieve your goals and we are sure that, as partners, we will create an ideal situation for everyone on your team to thrive.

Enjoy the month of tips and we hope to see you soon.

Thanks
MH

INTRODUCTION

If you picked up this book, you are probably in the car biz and, most likely, a service advisor. I have mad respect for folks in the car business. My Dad, Jack, has been "working on cars" for most of his life, and all of my life, first, as a mechanic on heavy-duty trucks in the late 70s and then as an owner of his own shop, *Jack's Truck Rigging*. The Texas oil bust of the early 80s gave me my first look at how the automotive business was cyclical and how difficult the job of navigating through those times could be. Ol' Jack landed on his feet though by turning wrenches again at another truck shop. Wasn't too long before he started his own independent car lot. *Jack's Cars and Trucks*. Now he was buying cars, fixing cars, selling cars and FINANCING CARS!

This is the part of the story where you would expect that I learned all about the car business from my dear old dad. You would be WRONG! I was a cocky little arrogant kid that only wanted to play video games all day. For some of you, that might sound familiar. Nope, young Mitch chose not to learn during this time. Instead, my dad passed along his knowledge to my brother Steve and lifelong friend, Jason.

During my training sessions, I often reference these three fellas as "Real Men" or "outside dawgs". You know what a "Real man" is don't you? A real man is one of those people that can bait a hook and skin a buck. A real man can hang sheet rock and make the lights come on. Outside dawgs are those that can live on their own without the help from others. An inside dog, like me, can't really do that. I cannot fend for myself. I need help. If you are a service advisor reading this book, YOU are a real man, or woman. You are tough. You are able to take the lumps of an up and down business and perform at a high level. Now what can an inside dog like me teach you? Well, some of what I watched my family do all of those years ago must have rubbed off.

Following a few years as a middle school math and history teacher, I have been in the "car business" for over twenty. I started

selling cars at a Ford store and rose through ranks. After nearly 10 years in the dealership world, I moved to MOC Products. My focus shifted to providing preventative maintenance products in Southeast Texas and Southwest Louisiana for a few years, before helping my company expand its territory nationally. For the past six years, my area of focus has been training. My specialty is helping people find their personal strength and making sure they show that strength to others. During my sessions, I like to share with each advisor that, "Greatness is inside each and every one of you. How often do you let that greatness out?" My job is to help you "let that greatness out".

In this book you will find "tips" that will allow you to let that greatness out. I want to give you tips that allow you to show each and every person you come in contact with the very best version of YOU. My tips will be simple, but not easy and they will not be technical. I will leave the technical aspects of being a service advisor to the "outside dawgs". I will not share with you what makes brake fluid break down or the difference in pistons or being pissed off. Instead, I will get into your shoes and your head and offer tips that you can use at work and at home.

I break these tips down into a calendar month. 31 days of tips that, I hope, help you during your month as a service advisor. I try to take into consideration, "where you are" during your month.

What are you thinking about in the first couple of days of the month? What should you be working on mid-month? What are "they" doing at a particular time of the month and are "they" affecting "you"? The book is best read in one day or in one-week sections. Ingest it a little at a time.

I use the word "they" a LOT in this book. "They"? Man, "They" are something. What in the world do "they" do all day, or week? Dang, it always seems like "they" have a leg up or that "they" seem to get whatever "they" want. How do "they" do it? That question is a mystery that will not be solved by reading this book. Instead of focusing on what "they" do, I want to present a series of tips that YOU can use to be "better".

I put "better" in quotation marks because "better", means

something different to everyone and "better" should be a moving target, especially if you are a service advisor. If you are a service advisor, be proud. Be proud that you are one of the few people that can do what you do, day in and day out. Be proud that you can "make a week of pay" in a day. Be proud that you are the captain of your own ship and you can set sail for the Bahamas, or crash your ship into the canal bank, if you choose...but I am getting ahead of myself and I have "talked" long enough. Let's get to work. It is the "First of the Month". What do you need to work on first? Turn the page and find out.

DAY #1: ATTITUDE

It is the first day of the month. Hopefully, you had a good month last month. Wait, I am not going to start off the month with such a weak proclamation. Hopefully, you had a good month? Hopefully??? Always remember, "Hope is not a strategy." That quote is from Rick Page, the author of a book with the same title. We are not going to begin on the basis of hope. So let's reboot.

It is the first day of the month and no matter if you flourished last month or languished, there is a new month in front of you. New customers to meet and greet and a new set of goals to smash and a new set of expectations that need to be exceeded. What should your first order of business be for the new month?

The tasks that you could begin your monthly work with seem endless and many of those tasks will be discussed throughout the book, but there is something that you need to get straight first.

Your ATTITUDE!

Having the right attitude is essential for your success. But what does that mean? What are some of the character traits that help define a great attitude? Let's take a look at a few traits and see if there are some attributes you can focus on that will allow you to create an optimal environment for creating YOUR great attitude.

Confidence
Imagination
Independent Thinking
Keen Observations
Dependability
Exuberance
Fearlessness
Positivity
Self-Motivated
Passion

I have found that the quickest way for a service advisor to capture a great attitude is to complete my "ONE thing" exercise.

Take your business card and turn it over to the blank side.

For the next 30 seconds or so, I want you to think about the ONE word that best describes why you are "valuable".   What ONE word best describes the essence of you? What ONE word sums up why you are a good spouse, parent, son or daughter or person in your community? What ONE word makes YOU, YOU?

Once you are able to break down your own essence, you can draw upon that attribute to create your ATTITUDE! Going back to the adjectives I listed above, are you confident in your essence? Does it drive you? It better. This trait is what you should want to put on display EVERY DAY!

Every time you speak to your boss, or a coworker, are you showing them what is at your core? Are you allowing your "best" version of yourself to grow or are you stunting the very thing that makes you valuable, that makes you special? Are you showing everyone the best version of yourself everyday?

It is the first day of a new month. Let's put your essence on display and let that propel your attitude to all time heights.

DAY #2: CONSISTENCY

Second day of the month. Objectives have been set and goals and benchmarks have been created. Where is your head? Are you ready to have a big month? You should have your attitude right from Day 1, but what do you do with your essence? How do you take that great attitude and put it to work? The answer: consistency.

For example, it has been widely reported that Michael Jordan wore the same University of North Carolina shorts during EVERY game he played as a professional. He felt that they brought him luck. The greatest player of his generation felt power in consistency.

Consistency, like MJ's, can take many forms. Habits, rituals, or superstitions are ubiquitous and take on many forms, but do they work and if so, why?

First, YES, they work. They work if you THINK they work because much of the effect is from within. Think about it. Who puts the most pressure on you in life? Who pats you on the back most often? To whom do you look to for guidance when you are down or where do you turn when you hear opportunity knocking? It better be that person that looks back at you in the mirror every morning! YOU!!! Shakespeare once quilled, "This above all; to thine own self be true."

Your habits will shape into a consistent form and through that consistency you will gain confidence. That confidence, in turn, will drive your essence and the attitude necessary to succeed. Let's go back to MJ.

Did those shorts give Jordan special powers? Not necessarily. But they did remind him of the work he put in to become great. They reminded him of the lessons and drills he learned over the first two decades of life that created the basketball god we all witnessed. They reminded him that the work was not done and that there was always a challenge in front of him. Those shorts reminded him of what he had already accomplished and what was left to accomplish.

What are the lessons and drills that you put yourself through

EVERY day to become the greatest service advisor in your company, your city, your state or the world? Are you choosing a consistent or ritualistic approach or do you go through each day willy-nilly? Unless your name is Willie Nilly, you better choose consistent.

As an advisor, consistency can be found everywhere. Look for these opportunities. Consistency can be found in your meet and greet and in your walk-around. Consistency is not only good for you but it is good for your customer. Consistency creates a palpable familiarity. Consistency can be found in your menus and in your inspection process. Consistency can be found in your active delivery or follow up process. Seek out your consistency today.

DAY #3: VALUE

Attitude, check. Consistency, check. It is Day #3 of your month. Where are your numbers through the first two days of the month? Have you had a big repair order yet? Don't get down if it is "slow" or you haven't "been lucky". We are going to create our own luck!

On the other hand, are you off to a great start? If so, don't get caught looking at the scoreboard and buying into the press clippings. Always remember, you are never as good as they think or as bad as they say you are.

My tip for Day #3 is: Value. Find the value, today. Find value in a product you have in your arsenal or value in a process or procedure that you do, and after you complete the task, share that value with EVERY person you come in contact with today.

The third day of your month is when you step into the shoes of your customers and think about, "What is in it for them?"(WIFT). So often during the race each month to perform at a high level, a service advisor is left to fend for themselves. What is inventory doing to YOU? What is the new pay plan doing to YOU? What is that new policy that "they" are trying to implement doing to "YOU"?

Let today be about WIFT. Let me elaborate. You have a new service to offer today. Let's say that this service is brand new to you and your store.

When you sell one of the new products, you make much more money than you would with a previous package or product that this service replaces. If the cost is the same, what is in the new package that was not available before? What is the value for THE CUSTOMER? That is what you need to focus on today. Another great example of value is your menu. What services do you have bundled and why are they bundled together? Today you must dig for that value and share that value with each and every person you come in contact with.

Again, let today be about, "What is in it for the customer?" Look deeper into your product list than normal today and see if you can find that diamond in the rough that you can use to dazzle your customers.

Think about value in terms of safety, performance, prevention or savings. Dig. Find the value in what you are offering to your customers.

DAY #4: TIMELINESS

Punctuality and awareness of time can help you gain respect with your customers. First, punctuality. Punctuality displays a person's respect for people and time and is an extension of the consistency tip from earlier. Showing the customer that you can get there when their doors open forges a bond between you and the customer. The simple act of showing up when they do shows that you share some of the same work experiences, and this will help you greatly when you need to ask more of them. However, you also need to be ready to do business when THEY are ready to do business. We all work different schedules, and you must be ready to accommodate the demands of your customer in order to get a deal done.

Next, awareness of time. You must be aware that particular times of the month or year are stressful to your customers and your managers. Be cognizant that the last few days, and first few days, of the month might not be the best times to meet with management or unload a new concept.

Similarly, get to know the patterns and driving habits of your customers. During the many appointments, throughout the years you work with customers, you should get to know them and take notes about your relationship. These notes could help you inform them about upcoming services. The more you know a customer, the more you can advise them.

Taking these notes and bringing that information up in conversation can impress your customers. Think about how great the customer will feel if you say, "By the way, how did your daughter's volleyball season go?" Timeliness and how aware you are of the time spent with a customer is invaluable. Remember, timing is everything.

As an advisor, one of the duties of your job is to be timely with your recommendations. You need to be aware of the time or mileage each service should be offered. You need to be aware of the length of time between the arrival of your customer and the time in which your multipoint inspection is complete. Timeliness is key, especially today.

DAY #5: PITCH THE POSITIVE

Whether you are discussing your maintenance products with a new customer or one that you have a longstanding relationship with, always pitch the positives first. Remember what almost every Mother around the world teaches children, "If you don't have something nice to say, don't say anything at all." Well, Mom is right. Always begin your pitch with a positive. Try to "reward action" not "punish inaction".

By sharing, first, that the service will help with performance of the vehicle, it allows the advisor to "pitch the positive" and not the negative. After the positive attribute of the service is given; then come back with the downside; not vice versa. An ounce of prevention beats a pound of cure, not the other way around.

Share with your customer that your product will help them in another area and leave the "avoiding disaster" comment for last.

Our culture today bombards us with negative, attack oriented, dog-whistle advertisements that are created to cause fear to the viewers. DO NOT FOLLOW SUIT! Studies have shown that creating sentiment with your product or through a relationship can be the most impactful way to have long lasting effects and sales. This sentiment is almost never created with negative origins.

While researching this topic a few words seemed to appear over and over.

Satisfy

Enhance

Strengthen

Each of these words is generally considered positive, and each is a term that you should incorporate in your daily vocabulary. Conversely, there are words that are used in ads and pitches that are clearly negative.

Trouble

Weaken

Cheap

Share with your customers how you and your products or

services can enhance or strengthen the things they already do well. Avoid telling them that you can help them with their weaknesses. Avoid telling your customers that the competition has cheap product. Instead, share with the customer how your product is a great investment. As an advisor, pitching the positive is an extension of the tip from Day #3: Value. There is much more value in the positive aspects of your recommendations than the negatives. Be positive with your customers today.

FIRST SATURDAY

Put down your PHONE!! OK, we are a bit into your month and I want to ask you to do something really, really difficult. It will be fine, I promise. But put down your damn phone. DON'T LOOK AT IT! I know you were just looking at it. DON'T! Study after study shows that putting down your phone and seeing the world through your eyes benefits you greatly. A few of those benefits:

Live Longer
Sleep Better
Increase Memory
Increase Productivity
Increase Decision Making
Decrease Stress
Decrease Obesity
Decrease Heart Attack Risk
Decrease Stroke Risk
Decrease Risk of Dementia

This tip is so important, I should have written about it for the beginning of the month. Beyond the effects listed above, putting down your phone and listening to your customers and family will help you sell more and feel better. Putting your phone in Do Not Disturb or Airplane Mode during discussions will be a huge benefit, as well. We can all hear when your phone is vibrating and that sound interrupts our conversation and is detrimental to the task at hand, so, do not shortcut by putting the phone on vibrate. Turn it off.

While we are on the topic of phones, update your voicemail daily. Many people today do not leave voice messages, but updating your message daily will decrease the number of call-backs from customers. If you share with them that you are out of the office until 2 p.m., they will not unnecessarily call you back at 12:30.

Never check your messages, text or voice, in the presence of a customer. It does them no good listening or watching you ignore them. It is rude and must be avoided at all costs.

Next, do not listen to your messages on speakerphone. You

never know what the message will uncover or who will be within earshot.

Finally, putting down the phone increases your chance to connect with people. That connection is vital to a service advisor. Selling is always personal and the more you connect with your customer on a personal level, the more you will sell.

Now, IT IS SATURDAY...get outside and have some fun!

FIRST SUNDAY

Compliment someone. We put the phone down yesterday, so today is a great day to start connecting with people and dishing out some compliments:

Appreciate
Being a team member or leader
Great example
Helpful
Kindness/thoughtfulness
Make a difference
Refreshing Perspective
Smart decision
Thanks for listening

Today, show someone your appreciation. Showing appreciation goes a long way. Showing and stating your appreciation to coworkers, customers and family creates a happy environment conducive to success. Happy team members create a stronger team, and happy customers will buy more and refer more business to you. Let people know that you appreciate them and let them know what you appreciate the most about them.

Tomorrow let one of your team leaders, or any member of your squad, know that you see them as a leader. Comments like this will allow you to lead by example and encourage other team members to do so as well.

So often leaders give the compliments but rarely do they get them in return. Being a leader is tough and just knowing that other team members see you as a leader is often motivation enough to stay one. Leaders need a pat on the back, too.

Compliment someone that offers kindness, thoughtfulness, or help. Just as we discussed in the previous paragraph, acknowledging a person who is leading by example or being kind or thoughtful will inspire them to continue this powerful behavior. In society today, we just are not as kind as we once were. The keyboard has jaded us and made us more inconsiderate and mean. When you see someone being thoughtful or kind, make sure they know it and that you appreciate them for doing so.

Share your pleasure when someone makes a difference to you, your work or your family life. No matter how large or small the significance is, merely recognizing that difference can make the day of someone else. Let people know that things wouldn't be as good without them. Be grateful.

You should look to compliment those that have a refreshing perspective. It is easy to become a part of "group-think", but it is often difficult to express a fresh idea or perspective. When you witness someone who does so, make sure to let him or her know that his or her actions are wanted and appreciated, even if the idea doesn't immediately take shape or make an impact.

Finally, compliment someone when you notice that they are actually listening or taking notes. Listening to someone is a selfless act and those that take pride in their listening are rarely acknowledged for having this skill. People who listen make great teammates and coworkers and would love to be complimented for their efforts.

DAY #6: KEEP IT SIMPLE

KISS is an acronym most popularly known for "keep it simple, stupid". Now, I certainly do not want to name call, so let's drop the stupid, and let's add a few "S" words that you can get traction from.

Keep it Simple

Keep it Silly

Keep it Straightforward

Keep it Short

First, Simple. The best plans are simple, not easy, but simple. These are oft-confused terms, simple and easy. Never challenge someone by saying that any change in his or her life, be it small or huge, is an easy one. Often as a service advisor when you describe something as "easy" it comes off extremely condescending. Another term to avoid when thinking of "keeping it simple" is basic. Referring to something as basic refers to it being remedial or entry level. Normally, not the feeling you want from your idea or product. Instead, keep it simple.

Next, keep it Silly. Whether you need an ounce or a pound of silliness, for most recipes of success, even a dash of silly can be helpful. Relationships between service advisor and customer are professional AND personal. Those relationships can be important AND lighthearted at the same time. The best relationships often have a little humor and silliness in them as well. Now, by no means am I suggesting that you have a comedy routine or become a clown with your customers. You can lose your credibility quickly with an ill-timed quip or comment, but inserting a little silliness can help bring down walls that are naturally erected between service advisor and customer.

For instance, wearing silly or colorful socks and ties can convey a degree of whimsy that can become a useful tool when you are presenting yourself or products. A bowtie certainly strikes the perfect balance of professional/personable.

Another KIS is Keep it Straightforward--straightforward in every sense of the word. First, look someone squarely in the eye. Meet a problem "head on". Also, an honest and straightforward presentation of facts about you or your product is essential. Do not go into a situation with an agenda. Finally, mean what you say and say what you mean. Any deviation from this can lead to problems on many levels.

Finally, Keep it Short. As you can tell with my style of writing, I personally believe strongly in keeping things brief and short. The more you talk, the more likely you are to talk yourself out of a sale. Share with your customers the essentials. Do not get lost in the weeds of detail. Often if you get too detailed, you will sound like a commercial. That is not a good thing. A favorite salesperson and friend of mine, Danny Ware, reminds me to this day that we are not selling the steak; we are selling the SIZZLE!

DAY #7: LISTEN ACTIVELY AND ACTIVELY LISTEN

Conversations dominate your sales life and livelihood. You have them with your boss, customers, prospective customers, and often yourself. During those many conversations, what is the percentage of time you spend listening, hearing, and speaking? Are you cognizant of the difference between listening and hearing? Today is the day that you work on your listening skills. During your conversations, work on the following:

Listen--do not just wait to speak.

Listen to people--don't just hear what they are saying.

Try to learn from the conversation by being attentive.

Summarize, but do not interpret or respond.

Give feedback.

As an advisor, you are trained and prepared for most of the objections that your customers throw at you on a daily basis. Often, that preparation can lead to you not listening to your customer but merely waiting until it is your turn to speak. Do not fall into that trap. While you might be fully capable of predicting what a person might say next, you are setting yourself up to miss vital details that make the current situation special. There will be plenty of time for you to overcome an impending objection or to head a problem off at the pass. My tip for you is to WAIT UNTIL THE OBJECTION IS STATED! Never assume.

A byproduct of waiting to speak instead of listening is that you are not only missing what people say, but, you also are not listening to their needs. Don't just hear; listen to a person and look for clues that will show you their wants and needs. Losing eye contact is a sign that you are not listening and your customer can pick up on those clues. When you are selling something, it should be YOU seeing clues, not the customer.

Listening requires you to be attentive. Paying attention during a conversation gives you the opportunity to learn. To learn what is really important to the customer and what isn't important is essential to your success. Nodding your head to affirm that you understand what they are saying and then looking for clues if this affirmation was welcomed are two things you can do. If they nod their head in return, that is a good sign. If they look at their feet, it is a bad sign.

After a customer has stated their concern or objection, you should summarize their position without interpretation or response. Avoid saying, "So what you mean is _____." Instead, merely summarize what they said and thank them for the information. "I appreciate you sharing that with me."

Finally, give some feedback and let them know what the next step is. If the conversation is negative, share with the customer what you can do to help remedy the concern. If the conversation was positive, speak to them about how you can build upon the conversation and how that will lead to the desired event...a sale.

DAY #8: BUILD RELATIONSHIPS

Maybe the best tip that you will read in this book is to always build relationships. From the kids you ate lunch with in sixth grade to your fraternity or sorority pledge class, the people that you meet throughout your life are your greatest support system and asset. You can keep those relationships alive through social media, shared activities like sports or hobbies, or quick phone calls and texts.

A few tips inside this tip:

Give them the deets

Ask questions and listen

Network

Sponsorships

First, when speaking of building relationships, it is all in the details. Share with people specifics about what you are doing, how you are doing, and how MUCH of it that you are doing. Give them specific examples of your challenges and listen to them when they offer suggestions. This makes them feel they are a small, albeit important, part of your process. It makes them more interested in seeing you succeed and that is a really good thing.

Next, ask specific questions about their business and listen to their responses. Normally misery loves company and success garners a parade. Be a part of both. When people share with you their struggles, let them know you understand. Avoid going tit-for-tat, however. It isn't a competition of who is struggling, or succeeding the most. On the contrary, when times are good for your associates, let them brag without sharing stories of your own success. Don't throw shade or belittle their wins, no matter the size of the accomplishment.

The next thing you need to work on is networking. From your favorite coffee shop and lunch table, wherever you go and whomever you see, everyone should know that you are THE service advisor in your field. Get to know the names and stories of everyone you meet and, again, pay attention to the details. You should know where the barista is attending college and how they are doing in class. You should know the tellers at the bank and whether or not they are trying to become a loan officer. You should know SOMETHING specific about them and they should know that when it comes to your product NOBODY could help them as much as you can. Remember, "Facts tell and stories sell!"

One of the best ways to network as a service advisor is a customer appreciation clinic. Help your manager organize an event that focuses, even more, on your customers. For instance, promote to your customers that every third Thursday of the month your store goes above and beyond for customers by hiring a fingernail technician for the day and everyone that does service that day can get a manicure. Let them know to bring a family member and mingle with everyone during this time. Remind all in attendance that you can help service ANY type of vehicle and that you would love for them to spread the word about you and your store.

Always remember, your goal is to boost awareness in YOUR business. Take a moment near the beginning of the gathering for an announcement to promote your business.

Two more thoughts when planning your event: Set a budget and stick to it and create a buzz about your event on social media. Also, make sure you live tweet during your event to help the buzz continue until your next gathering.

DAY #9: NEVER CRITICIZE DIGITALLY

Times have changed and the preferred method of contact for most people is some form of digital communication. Text, email, messenger, phone apps, social media--the list of ways to communicate with customers is a long one indeed. All of these can be used effectively as a service advisor, but under NO circumstances should you use them to criticize, bash, or communicate condescendingly to your customers.

First, always be careful of how you structure a digital message. Often, an unintended attitude can be read into your message. Just state facts when texting a customer and leave your opinions for conversations by phone.

Another common situation occurs when a customer criticizes you or one of your products online. The person may claim that they got a much better deal from one of your competitors. Instead of lashing out at the customer and telling them what THEY could have done to do business with you, let them know instead of what YOU could have done differently.

Next, to be safe, if you have something to communicate that could be construed in any way, as negative, call the person on the phone or meet with them in person. The keyboard is a powerful tool and often makes us feel emboldened when it concerns our personal views. In person, your views and opinions are often softened. The likelihood that you take an objection and turn it around in person is much greater than attempting to do this in a quick text format.

Finally, always be aware of the screenshot evidence of a poor decision you made, in anger or frustration, toward a customer. Once you digitally send someone a negative message, they can hold that evidence forever.

Emily Dickinson wrote, "A word is dead when it is said, some say. I say it just began to live that day." Well, words that are texted or posted live forever! Do not let the archives of your words be negative.

DAY #10: PROOFREAD EVERYTHING!

I must admit, most of these tips are mine but this one is not. My wife is the Proofreader in Chief and she finds mistakes everywhere. She finds them on television graphics, on church handouts, on restaurant menus, and in just about everything I complete. Each time she does, she remarks how she loses a little respect for those involved. Proofreading takes only a few additional moments, but will elevate your communications greatly.

Read your text aloud
Read your text slowly
Read your text silently
Use the tools
Use your friends and coworkers

Begin your proofreading by reading your text aloud, just as if you were presenting it in a meeting or speech. If there were any words that need to be emphasized, check to see if a comma would help create a pause but stay grammatically correct. Avoid using bold font or ALL CAPS to generate emphasis. Both of these methods often create unintended emotion for the reader.

Next, read your text slowly and concentrate on each word. Focusing on every word will force you to analyze the intended meaning of each sentence. Be aware of your choice of words and pick words and phrases to match your intended audience. For instance, do not use industry jargon when corresponding with customers.

You should also read your text silently and use this time as an opportunity to focus on punctuation. Try to read every word in each sentence and not just scan the document. Take the time to analyze the document as a whole and make sure that the spacing and justification look professional.

When proofreading your document, take advantage of each tool available to you. *Spellcheck, Grammatik, Grammarly*, and *Hemmingway* are all Apps and tools that you should investigate. Pick the tool that works best for you and run the program or App on each correspondence you create.

Finally, use your friends and coworkers to put another set

of eyes on your writing. Sometimes you think you are being clear and concise, but others may not agree. While most people are not skilled in proper grammar usage, you can find their insights on content very helpful. A great tip is to have them share with you what they thought your meaning and intention of the correspondence was. This will let you know if you properly conveyed your message.

SECOND SATURDAY: KNOCK, KNOCK, KNOCK

It is time to prospect! Well, every day is a great day to prospect, but you should get your plan on paper today and make
a commitment to yourself to prospect for new customers wherever you go!

Start with:

*Small circles, like Friends and Family

*Your community

*Small community events

*Sponsor youth organizations

*Businesses you frequent

The first person you must prospect is yourself. YOU should
always purchase your own product or service. Amway is a multi-
level marketing company that sells household goods that started
in 1959. The very first thing it teaches/preaches to its members
is to change their personal buying habits and start buying items
from themselves instead of the local market. The mindset that
Amway instills is that if you can master the servicing of your
OWN household, and see the tangible benefits that Amway can
provide, you will become more knowledgeable and passionate
about the products and program, and those feelings will spread
throughout your circle. Your product or service is no different.
The first person that should be onboard with what you are selling,
is YOU!

Once you have convinced yourself that your product is worth
something, it is time to move on to your circle of family and
friends. Your small circle of "people" that you can practice your
speech, pitch, or delivery on. These people are invaluable to the
overall growth of your business. Your friends and family should
be able to pitch products for you to their friends and family because they should be experts when you are finished with them!

Another benefit from starting the prospecting process with
the people you know is that they often give you brutally honest
feedback. There are few people as willing to cut you down at the
knees than the crazy uncle at a BBQ. You should listen to even HIS
criticism. Remember, behind most criticism is a grain of truth or

perception. Take your lumps here and get better.

Finally, remember that the average person knows 600 people. If you can impress your family and friends, they, in turn, can greatly increase your potential customer base. More on Networking in a later chapter.

The next circle you must draw is around your community. Be friendly to your neighbors by waiving, and don't forget to "press the flesh". Get involved in civic associations. Put signs in your yard promoting local businesses and become one of the local businesses that others support. You should be the preeminent expert and salesperson of your product in your neighborhood. Everyone on your block needs to know what you are offering and why you are the best.

Own your old high school or college. Be an active alumnus and give money back to the kids whenever you get a chance. Also, try to document your involvement and post those pics, when appropriate, on your social media sites. You do not need to pound your chest when you do something good for someone else, but you do not need to keep it a secret either.

The next circle should encompass the businesses you frequent. Can you sell your products to businesses that you patronize? How about the people that work at those businesses, like the waitress, cashier, or your mechanic? There are prospective customers everywhere. Let me give you a personal example.

I have worked in the automotive industry for over 20 years and most of the customers we have are automotive dealerships and facilities. We sell everything from oil to paper plates and trash bags. When I do training after hours, I often buy my attendees dinner and BBQ at one of my favorite spots. Recently I spent a few days in Texas and bought Rudy's BBQ three nights in a row. On the third night, the manager came up to me to say thank you and noticed the packets that I was preparing at a back table. I let him know that I was a sales trainer for an oil company and that the food was for my trainees. Within 90 seconds, the manager asked me what else I sold and within five minutes, he gave me a list of items that I could sell him.

Even I was not looking for a new customer that night, but I still got one! Customers are everywhere and it is your job to make sure that they all know that YOU are the service advisor for them.

SECOND SUNDAY: GET YOUR MIND RIGHT

"True change is within; leave the outside as it is."—Dalai Lama
OK, the end of the month is approaching and you have a few more days to hit that bonus, reach that next percentage and make the money that you have worked so hard for this month. My tip today is take a few minutes and get your mind right.

*Meditate
*Exercise
*Music
*Passion
*Goals

Many successful people, like Oprah for example, feel that even three minutes of meditation per day help immensely. Doctors agree. Daniel J. Siegel of UCLA says this about three minutes of meditation, "Just as people practice daily dental hygiene by brushing their teeth, mindfulness meditation is a form of brain hygiene—it cleans out and strengthens the synaptic connections in the brain." While a plethora of books exist to give you ideas, it is all about replacing the stress of a long month with a few minutes of relaxation.

For those of you that feel a little more frisky, exercise can clear the mind as well. Early morning jogs or a quick workout at lunch or hitting the heavy bag tonight-- indulge today in your favorite vigorous activity. The trick to this is to not think about work during your "work" out. Trust me, focus on your Jay-Z or Billie Eilish tune and escape the daily grind for a bit. You will come out feeling fresh and ready to attack the remainder of your month.

While we are on the topic, there may be no better way to get your mind right than with the power of music. From jazz, rap, country, or metal and anything in between, find music that you can get lost in. Today is about getting out of your head and clearing it of anything else. Find a tune that you can sing and sing it LOUDLY!!! At the end of your favorite song this morning you should be envisioning yourself onstage with an audience in the palm of your hand.

If chilling out and meditating isn't your cup of tea and you just do not have a song that you can exercise to, I have one more suggestion. What are you most passionate about? Family? A hobby? Whatever impassions you, take a few minutes and focus on that today. These are the things that we have been working toward all month any way. Allow yourself a few minutes today to realize that all of this work will pay off soon.

Finally, if you can't totally escape your mind, then during any of these activities today, stay focused on your number one goal whatever that may be. Envision yourself hitting that goal, making that sale or reaching new heights. Close your eyes and really try to see yourself being successful. Remember, your greatest opponent is YOU. Clear your head today and end the month strong.

DAY #11: PRODUCT KNOWLEDGE

Know your product and make sure you know your product much more than your customers do. Take today and learn something new about your product. Your customers yearn for product knowledge. Let's give it to them!

Be thorough and gain product knowledge from many angles. Learn how your product is seen through the eyes of customers, competition and your coworkers. You should talk to your friends and family and ask them how they see your product. All of this research on product knowledge will enhance your performance as a service advisor.

First, you will gain confidence. The more knowledge you have about your product the more confident you will become in presenting it to customers. Confidence, of course, pays huge dividends in sales and you will exude more confidence with the more you learn. Essentially, the more you learn the more confident you become. The more confident you become the more you sell. The more you sell, the more you will want to learn and that creates a "Success Cycle". Ride that success cycle!

Let that confidence come out in the form of articulate and professional communication. You should know so much about your product that you could give a speech in front of thousands of prospective customers and, rest assured, they will all leave impressed. When you begin to communicate like a pro, your enthusiasm will become robust and you will be able to overcome objections easier, which will lead to more sales.

Next, I know you will hate this one, but next, you need to role-play. Learn something new about your product and then role-play with a coworker. This exercise should lead to more learning, and by gaining the knowledge of your coworker, you can get even better. Role playing and practicing your sales craft are necessary and an extremely healthy way to grow as a sales professional.

You should spend some time each month on the investment and value of your goods/services. Work on knowing what your competitors' prices are and why yours is what it is; more importantly, though, know the VALUE of your product. While we are at it, take the words "price" and "cost" out of your vocabulary today and replace each of them with "investment". The logic behind this switch is simple. If I shared with you that my daughter had braces and I thought they were pretty "pricey", do you think we paid a little or a lot? If I share with you that my grandfather fought in a "costly" battle, did a few people die or a lot? In each of these examples, you would answer "a lot". So, instead of saying the price of your product is $575, say that the "total investment" would be $575. "Total Investment" feels much lower than a "price". Finally, on that note, do not say "grand total" because a "grand total" sounds much larger than "total".

Learn the history of your product. People love to connect products with something from their past, or the past of a loved one. Know when your product, or products, debuted and use this to connect with your clients. People dig nostalgia and, if your product is current, push the idea that the product is innovative. Either way, try using the debut date to connect with your client.

You also need to learn about how your products are created, manufactured, or cultivated, whatever the case may be. Knowing your product means having knowledge about its origin throughout its creation, production, and ending with that product being offered to your client. Again, pay attention to the details. It's all in the deets!

Master how to use your product and be able to share tips about ongoing maintenance or future information that will enhance the customer's experience. A master service advisor knows how to demonstrate the product and keep the customer engaged while doing it.

Finally, know the benefits of your product and not just the features. Do not share that your suit has three pockets. Show your customer what can fit into them. SHOW, not TELL! Remember, the difference between features and benefits: Features are what your product HAS and benefits are what is in it for the customer.

I am from an automotive professional background and that is where I found my best example of features and benefits.

"Don't tell me what's in it for the car...tell me what's in it for the customer." Take that mindset and apply it to your business, and you will sell more product.

DAY #12: ASK FOR FEEDBACK, AND LISTEN

We are midway through the month and today's tip is about listening, learning, and introspection. Today, you should ask for feedback from customers, coworkers, and friends. The most difficult part of the tip is listening. Here is a list of do's and don'ts when getting feedback.

*Do not react-- ACT

*Do not shoot the messenger or yourself

*Say Thank You

*Do not take it personally

*Do not view mistakes as failures

First, we need to listen without reacting. Instead of reacting negatively, act responsibly and create a plan of action instead of reacting and creating a debate or a drama. Most service advisors will go on the attack when they receive criticism. We want to squash the discussion entirely instead of taking a moment and listening to the concern. You must reverse this trend.

That being said, we should never shoot the messenger. Many times you will get feedback via a third party or a concerned friend or coworker. Remember, these people are only trying to help. There is no reason to unnecessarily bite someone's head off. Keep your cool. Also, do not let criticism get you down. Do not beat yourself up over it. Instead, take criticism in stride and use it to get better. Even if you have been misunderstood, misquoted, or you feel the criticism is down right wrong, dig deep and find the grain of truth. Shakespeare penned, "To thine own self be true..." If only it were that easy!

Take time and thank those that give you feedback, either positive or negative feedback. Always remember that normally people feel awkward giving feedback in the first place, so make sure they know that you appreciate the effort and that you will act upon it. For any industry where survey data is collected, take the time to send a message of thanks, letting the client know that you received the survey. If possible, make a note in their account in your DMS, and personally thank them upon return to your business. The client will then realize that their efforts are genuinely remembered. That is a really good thing.

Next, "It's not personal, it's business." This quote was uttered a few times in the Godfather circa 1972, and it is still true today. Always keep in mind that most feedback is about business, not about you as a person. Even if the criticism is spot on and you deserve negative feedback, that one interaction does not define you as a person. Never let criticism get you down. The toughest opponent to beat is you. The essence of that last sentence has been printed on a myriad of posters and pages. Get one. Put it on your desk or workstation and live it each day. YOU are the only thing standing in the way of your success. Never let criticism get to YOU because it will make that fight even tougher.

And with that, we will finish this chapter with some great inspirational quotes about feedback and failures:

"One fails forward to success."—C.S. Lewis

"Only those who dare to fail greatly can ever achieve greatly."—Robert Kennedy

"Criticism, like rain, should be gentle enough to nourish a man's growth without destroying his roots."—Frank A. Clark

"It's very important to have a feedback loop, where you're constantly thinking about what you've done and how you could be doing it better."—Elon Musk

DAY #13: WORK YOUR PAY PLAN

If you are like most service advisors you are on commission, and often, are on a pay plan where you get a draw against your commissions. That is why today's tip is about working your pay plan.

The middle of the month is a great time to check on what you are selling and what you are on pace to sell for the month. When doing so, make sure you are aware of any bonuses or SPIFF that you are within reach of.

First things first. Know your pay plan. Does your pay plan have escalators that kick in when you reach higher sales levels? Does your pay plan contain fast start or fast finish bonuses? Close out your ROs! You don't get paid if a ticket isn't closed.

Next, are you selling EVERYTHING or just the big stuff? Many times this is the case for Main Shop Advisors. Don't just wait on the big engine or transmission job to come along. Take a close look at each opportunity and offer EVERYTHING a customer needs, not just their primary concern. There is a ton of money to be made selling the extras, so you better sharpen ALL of your skills and not just the skills that push your primary jobs.

With the expansion of items, you need to track the sales of each item. If you have 20 different items that you can sell, create a chart that lists all 20 items and then place an "X" in the chart each time you sell one. The best way to maximize your earning potential is to sell a little bit of everything, instead of focusing on a few items. You should never go a week without selling ONE of a certain item. I have met with thousands of service advisors and I will ask them "What is the number one reason why you haven't sold a brake fluid exchange all week?"

"Because I haven't asked?" is always the response. You gotta ask for the business, on everything, or you will never get it.

When you become a more balanced service advisor and you start selling a little bit of everything, try to get a "crooked" number for each reporting period. What am I talking about? Not a 1 or a zero for a certain product on any given day. Give me another number of sales on a particular item. You can sell me two alignments instead of one. You can sell me three sets of wipers in a weekend, instead of one. Give me a crooked number. If you do, working your pay plan will start being a lot more fun!

DAY #14: FOLLOW UP

Another big tip day. You MUST have a clear follow-up strategy and purpose for each follow up. While there are many follow-up plans available to you, choose a program that suits your business well. Remember, there are many ways to follow up with customers: phone, email, text, social media and snail mail. The best follow-up strategies will use a few of these elements and not just focus on one way to reach out to your customers.

Once you choose a strategy, be persistent and consistent. What's the difference you might ask? Consistency is behaving or acting the same way or doing something the same way over time, while persistency is doing the same thing while overcoming difficulties and challenges. Few of your customers will admit that they desire any follow-up, but almost every customer will feel that you care when you do reach out to them.

So, search independently on a follow-up process that you can get behind and in the event you get stuck, I would like to share my method with you. I call it 22-22.

2 Hours

2 Days

2 Weeks

2 Months

Yes, you read that right. I suggest that you follow up with EVERY customer two hours after your initial meeting ends.

This initial, two-hour follow up is best done electronically. Using a template email or text that reminds the customer of what you and your service or goal is, along with a small detail about your meeting that will show the customer that you were listening.

For instance, "(Customer Name), Thank you again for visiting with me about life insurance today. Here at (business name), we stand for Truth Through Transparency, and I personally believe that we have a plan that will accommodate the needs for you and your family. After discussing the programs with (Spouse's Name), feel free to reach out to me for any other details you might need."

I love when service advisors share their company's mission

statement in the first follow up. Doing so should reiterate the strength of your company and, hopefully, one of the reasons the customer visited the establishment in the first place! Remember your Phil Long 5 Ps! Start with "People" and during your follow up; reiterate how important each and every customer is to YOU!

The two-day follow up should be done face-to-face, by video-conference, or on the phone. During this contact you need to establish if the customer is still in the market for your goods or service, as well as restating their primary objection and/or cause for hesitation. Be prepared for this call by speaking to any other manager or supervisor that you have in your company and focus on any concessions or discounts that you can give to the customer to entice them to return. Normally, you only have one or two chances to close someone, so have your ducks in a row BEFORE you make the call. The last thing you want to occur during your call is have the customer ask you for a concession that previously held up the deal and you respond with, "Well, let me get with my manager." The two-day gap is the time to get with a manager. This follow up is your time to shine. To be the "Hero of the deal"! Get the people back and SELL THEM SOMETHING!

In many retail situations, if you have not closed the deal in 48 hours, someone else has, but you still need to reach out to the customer and check. In this email, you need to focus on the customer. List any details that you noted from your meetings and GET PERSONAL. If they have purchased somewhere else, you might be able to, at the very least, plant a seed for a future sale. More importantly, if they have not purchased, this email should show them that you listened and cared.

"(Customer Name), Hope things are going well for you and (Spouse Name). Have you made a decision? I remember that getting a policy over 1 million was essential to you because of your ever-growing responsibilities. Family is the most important thing in our lives and if you are ready to protect them, I am here to help. If fate took you elsewhere, thanks for giving me a chance to be a part of your journey. If not, make me aware of anything stopping you from doing business with me."

Hope, responsibility, family, protections, fate, journey and awareness are words that evoke emotion and the usage of these words at this juncture of your follow-up is ideal.

Finally, the two month follow-up can be done via email or snail mail. This contact is similar to the two-hour contact. Reiterate the strength of you and your company, but end with any information that is pertinent to your deal. Rebates, discounts, and financing options that might not have been available two months ago that are currently available to the customer would be perfect.

"(Customer Name), Hope things are going well in your search for life insurance. Our Truth Through Transparency programs are chosen by scores of customers each day, so I would love to find one that works best for you and yours. "Since we met two months ago, there have been a few rate reductions that could make your decision to choose, today, even better. As always, I am there for you if needed."

Two hours, two days, two weeks and two months. Be persistent and consistent when following up with your customers. If you do, you will see a big difference in your income.

DAY #15: DOCUMENT

So often in our work lives, we get so caught up in what we are doing that we lose track of time. We are so busy that we do not take a few moments to document where we are, where we have been and where we are going. We become the proverbial "chicken with their head cut off". Today's tip is a reminder to take a breath and document. I promise, it will save you SO much time and anguish in the future.

I know, I know. Slow down and take your time is not a tip that you think you can take heed. I get it. Out of all of the tips I have written about, this is the toughest one for me personally. In school, I was always the first one finished. I didn't take quality notes and I was a "speak first and listen last" kind of guy. When I was younger and had few responsibilities, I could manage my affairs by dropping everything else and focusing on what needed to be done right then and there. As my responsibilities grew, sadly, so did my mistakes. My performance would suffer because I just could not keep up with everything I needed to do. The following list of ways to document what you have done and what you need to do will keep you ultra-productive and on top of your success:

*To do list
*Green, Yellow, Red self-performance charts
*Emails to yourself
*Calendar Reminders/Outlook
*Read Receipts
*Hard calendar
*Before, during and after pics
*Videos

First things first, create a To Do list. Start your list with things that you need to do each day to be successful. On my personal list, I have "Drink 64oz of water" and "Get Cardio". Your To Do list does not need to be solely "work related". Being of a healthy mind, body, and soul will create a personal work environment that is conducive for success. Next, I like to use my Green, Yellow, and Red scale for my list. When I complete a task, I mark it green and when I fail to do so, I mark it red. I use yellow for instances when I complete a task, but maybe not at 100% effort: say, when I do 20 minutes of cardio instead of 45.

Next, I email my list to myself at the end of each week. This gives me documentation about what I did that week and I use this when questions arise about it or when I completed a certain task. Again, for instance, if you were tasked by your boss to file paperwork or work on your open R/O list, it could come in handy to be able to tell them, "Yes, I filed paperwork last Thursday. Here is a copy of my email when I completed that task." Having documentation like that can save your hide! More on that in a bit. Also, when you send a customer or coworker an email, make sure your emails are saved in your "Sent" file or CC yourself on the email. Again, having documentation on that communication can be very useful.

When scheduling tasks or meetings for others, it is best that you use a system that documents this, such as Outlook. When you create an event in Outlook, it goes on your calendar and that date is normally saved on each of your devices. Set up a reminder; say an hour before your event, where you are given notice on your phone or device reminding you of the upcoming appointment. Some people use 15 minutes, but I feel that if the reminder does catch you off guard, 15 minutes might not be enough time to prepare for the event. Try a one-hour reminder system and adjust accordingly.

Another thing you can do to document your work is to send emails with "Read Receipts" attached. The only warning I will give you on this is that it can annoy the recipient, but there are times where documentation trumps everything else. Read receipts will normally alert the recipient to the idea that you are documenting the thread and can sometimes change their behavior towards the intended task. I normally only use this with people that I do not already have a trusting relationship.

If spreadsheets and online calendars are not your thing, do not be afraid to just use an old school monthly calendar. I know plenty of successful people that keep a desk-sized calendar complete with to do lists, prospects and appointments. Business worked for decades without the Internet and you can be successful without it, too. If you take this approach, I highly urge you to keep the hard copies in a file for safekeeping and evidence. Just like before, if the boss asks you when you completed the filing task, having your calendar, as evidence will help prove you completed the task in a timely manner. Use a phone call log to document your customer interaction.

Taking before, during, and after pictures, or videos, can help document your progress in a fun manner and those photos can be used for prospecting, networking and building relationships. If you post pictures to your social media outlet, this also time stamps when you were doing specific aspects of your tasks. Videos and pictures are time stamped and are the ultimate documentation of your work. Just like in the examples above, you will have proof that you did what you say you did WHEN you said you did it!

THIRD SATURDAY: UPDATE YOUR CONTACT LIST

Take some time out today and update your contact list. First, your contact list must be thorough and include some interesting tidbits about the person that you can use during your follow-up:

First and Last name
Nickname or Title
Email address
Mailing address
Cell phone number
Date met
Place met
Product interested in
Interesting tidbit
Notes from meeting

The importance of the above information cannot be understated. You need to document as many details about your contact as possible and use this information during your follow-up schedule. My favorite part of this contact list is the interesting tidbit. This can be a hobby that you learned through conversation, or hot button item that you could use in the future. Remembering something special about your customer or prospective customer will impress them when you recall that item. This mindset can be seen in waitresses, waiters, and baristas around the country. How impressed are you when you return to Starbucks and the barista asks, "Triple Venti Skinny Vanilla Latte?" or when they simply write your name on your cup without asking. Recalling details like this separates a person that works in sales and a true service advisor.

Next, use social media to find new customers and add to expand your circle of contacts. When you post information or videos to your page, reach out to any person that likes, shares or retweets your content. Talk to them about your products and ask them about what aspects intrigue them the most.

Group your contacts or segment the list to better use the information. If you have the capability, store your contacts in a data base program. For instance, if you list the products that a person was interested in, you can just send texts or emails to those people about those particular products. This will save you time and energy and will also keep you in good standing with that person. Nobody wants to get emails about a truck when they were interested in a convertible. Don't waste your time or your customer's time.

Finally, take and keep notes each time you interact with a customer or future customer and be able to reference those notes during a personal follow-up later. You should be able to quickly get back to where you left off with a prospective customer and be able to speak about a current customer in detail. The only way to accomplish this is with notes. I take notes during meetings and training sessions on my phone. I inform everyone present that I am taking notes on my phone to avoid them getting the wrong impression and I often recap my personal notes with the person. Doing this helps me be more transparent and then the notes I took are added to my contact list later.

While this process may seem to be time consuming, adding notes to your contact list will generate revenue down the road.

THIRD SUNDAY: DO NOT GOSSIP

I am sure, as you have read through the first few chapters, that I want to share with you things TO DO and avoid telling you what NOT TO DO! Pitch the positive, be on time; and create value, are all positive things to work on; however, the theme for this chapter is a DON'T DO! DO NOT GOSSIP. Unknown in origin but a nonetheless spot on quote, "Anyone who will gossip to you, will gossip about you." Time and time again, I have seen people engage in a passive form of gossip that comes back to haunt them.

For example, a normal gossip session can be as innocent as this.

Coworker: "Man, I can't believe Eric makes everyone complete those forms. Can you believe that guy?"

You: "Nah, man."

The next week, Eric calls and questions you about a conversation you had about the form. The person you spoke with told Eric that you couldn't believe he makes everyone fill out those forms!

Eric asks why you would say that and you are in the doghouse.

Instead of sitting idly by and being part of a gossip session, provide solid, positive counsel. Let's take the same conversation and avoid gossip while maintaining our positive relationship with everyone involved.

Client: "Man, I can't believe Eric makes everyone complete those forms. Can you believe that guy?"

You: "Have you tried talking to him? I'm not saying complain to him, but really talk to him? Let him know how this is affecting YOU. Make it about YOU, not the form."

All of the advice you gave in the above response is constructive and very few people would have a problem with you speaking candidly and honestly.

Finally, NEVER be the origin of a gossip session. You have absolutely no reason to engage in a negative conversation with anyone in your company. Nothing positive comes from gossip and should be avoided entirely.

English historian Thomas Buckle once said, "Great minds discuss ideas. Average minds discuss events. Small minds discuss people." Exercise your great mind and don't stoop to small mindedness.

DAY #16: USE TECHNOLOGY

The tip for today is for those that are tech savvy and those that are still attached to the desk calendar. You must use technology to help sell your product. Without the use of technology in your process, you are most likely capping your effectiveness and your commissions.

*Texts

*Videos

*Live Streaming

The first is essential. Start by getting permission from your customers to text them, and follow that up with pertinent texts. As we covered during the follow-up chapter, sending a text a few hours after you meet someone and a couple of days later gives you a platform that insures the information you want to be delivered is done quickly and cheaply. You can also send pictures via text if the situation arises.

The next bit of technology that you need to become more comfortable with using is video. In many industries, video can replace some common paperwork. For instance, in the automotive industry, multi-point inspections have been carbon copy paperwork for decades. However, in the past few years they are being replaced with a video from your certified technician showing the technician working on your car and pointing out causes for concern. If a picture is worth a thousand words, then a video is worth tens of thousands. Also, remember that you do not need to be the star of the video; let your product be the star. You can video your product and just be the narrator.

Finally, live streaming you and your product can be very powerful. If you have connected with your customers via social media, live streaming brings immediacy to your presentation and gives you an easy way to market yourself and your product to the masses, again, quickly and cheaply.

Embrace technology and find the medium that best suits you and your product.

DAY #17: READ ABOUT SALES

I guess this could have been tip #1! If you are this deep into my book, I want to say thanks. I hope this material is making you think and is making you act upon those thoughts, but this cannot be the last book you read about sales. Always have a book or two that you are reading and make sure that those books are coming from different perspectives of the sales spectrum.

*Psychology of sales
*Sales methods
*Classic salespeople
*Cutting edge salespeople
*Hands on and habits
*Left field sales

Read books about the psychology of sales. This group of sales books normally focuses on YOU: what you can do to help yourself sell and what helps you get out of your own way when you are not selling. Psychology of sales books go deeper into the relationship building aspects of sales and less into the "To Do" list ideas like mine. If YOU impress people, they buy YOU and not your product. A great example of this is, *You, Inc.: The Art of Selling Yourself* by Harry Beckwith & Christine Clifford Beckwith. These are good books to read when you are really rolling.

The most popular sales books are the ones that help you hone your sales method skills. ZIG ZIGLAR! *The Secrets of Closing the Sale* gave us "The ABC's of sales" and "Stop Selling, Start Helping". Sales method books dive a little bit deeper into the process of the sell and become a bit more granular than the psychology of sales. This category of sales books works very well for the new service advisor or when you hit a slump.

Next, the classics. *Secrets of Closing the Sale* by Ziglar, *How to Win Friends and influence People* by Dale Carnegie and *How I Raised Myself From Failure to Success in Selling* by Frank Bettger are three that instantly come to mind. Like many aspects of our world today, we often forget about the classics. So much can be learned by looking back and not always focusing on the future. These classics are the reason I advised you to always be reading a book or two. Mix in a classic sales book with any of the categories and let the wisdom wash over you!

While the classics are essential, times change and customers evolve, so we, as service advisors, must stay fresh with our approach. To do so, I suggest reading the latest and greatest in sales books by today's best authors. *Eat Their Lunch!* by Anthony Lannarino, *Sales EQ: How Ultra High Performers Leverage Sales-Specific Emotional Intelligence to Close the Complex Deal* by Jeb Blount, and *Drive* by Daniel Pink are all very good reads that focus on the customers of today.

Try to stay fresh with your personal sales process by reading books that help with your habits and give "hands on" advice and tips. This book is a perfect example of things that you can do everyday to drive the success that so many people write about. Books like mine and *New Sales. Simplified.: The Essential Handbook for Prospecting and New Business Development* by Mike Weinberg give you exercises and information that you can use, on the job, to become a better service advisor.

Finally, an essential way to expand your sales horizons is to find stories and industries that are not normally thought of as "sales oriented" and learn out of the box tricks of the trade. I call these left field sales. Without question, my favorite book in this category is Coach Wooden's *Pyramid of Success* by John Wooden. My, oh my, what a book. In this category, I look for highly successful people and take bits and pieces of what made them successful and implement those pieces into strategy of life. I gravitate to sports, but you can find success in so many areas: military, culinary, music, and parenthood. Read about the success of others and implement what you can into your own life.

DAY #18: PLAN AND PREPARE

Spend the last 15 minutes of each workday planning for the next day: Again, ol' Ben Franklin: "If you fail to plan, you are planning to fail." Map out your route for the next day. Make sure that you meet tomorrow on your terms. Today's tip is about planning and preparation for your tomorrow, every tomorrow, today.

*Write your notes
*Group your small tasks
*Clear your desk
*Clear your inbox
*Quick study of your calendar
*Get ready for the first hour tomorrow

First, throughout each day you should be jotting down notes and action items to create a "To Do" list. Keeping detailed notes creates many sales opportunities and those notes are crucial, as you have read, in building relationships with your customers. If you take note on your phone, make sure that you share that detail with your customers. A customer could get offended if they think you are playing on your phone instead of working for them. Just be open and transparent about taking notes and you will be fine. While you create your "To Do" list, group your smaller tasks at the top of the list. Easily knocking out small items early during your day will create a greater sense of accomplishment as your day progresses.

Next, clear your desk of clutter, especially once you have completed a task. File account information properly and make sure that you secure confidential items immediately. Do not leave sensitive information visible to others at any time during your sales process. Customer data is sensitive and must be treated as such.

Very similar to your actual desktop, keep your inbox clear and your desktop on your computer organized as well. Create folders and label them properly. Organizing your email and computer desktop will make finding important information later much easier. Again, if you keep digital copies of private customer information, make sure you password protect those files. A password tip: Make your password a nonsense phrase. For example, ClownPhilly@Steak. Using upper and lower case, along with a symbol has become a standard requirement for many sites.

After you clear your digital desktop, study your upcoming calendar. Again, add any notes, big or small, that you feel my help give you an edge. Send out appointment confirmations and calendar reminders to anyone that you are expecting to join you. You just can't be thorough enough when planning.

Finally, take the last 15 minutes of your workday solely to prepare for your next day of work. Again, concentrate on the necessary items needed to complete those first smaller tasks on your list. Think about whom you will see and always highlight your biggest meeting of the day. Few things are as important as prepping for that big meeting or customer visit you have scheduled for tomorrow. Visualize your plan and preparation, culminating in the big sale that will make your month in the final few days.

DAY #19: GOAL SETTING

Today is the day where we put our goals on paper and set a plan for the future. The future, of course, is now, so our goals need to be immediate; but not so short-sided that we fail to see the forest for the trees. Make sure you write down your goals. Studies have shown that you are 80% more likely to hit your goals if you write them down. Now, before you start writing down and setting your goals, make sure that each of them has the following traits.

*Goals are Measurable

*Goals are Trackable

*Goals are Attainable

First, measurable. Your goals must be measurable. If not, then they are merely aspirations. For instance, as a coach, I asked my "kids" to set goals for a bench pressing max. When my players turned in their goal sheets, I had many write down that they wanted to be "the strongest I can be". While that is nice, it is not a goal. A goal would be that they want to bench 300 pounds. 300 pounds is measurable and "strong as can be" is not. So, create goals that are measurable.

Second, your goals must be trackable, and YOU need to track them. We will discuss this in the next chapter. Tracking your goals is essential. If you do not know where you are, how do you know how you are going to get where you want to be?

Finally, your goals must be attainable. If you currently sell 22 services a month, do not set your monthly goal for 50 services. Set small incremental increases. Set challenging, but reachable, goals.

The quest for the next goal gets easier with each milestone you reach. Building your gross from $60,000 a month to $64,000 a month and then $70,000 will get you accustomed to reaching your goals and that will make your next goal easier to reach. That brings us to the next task. Break your goals down into the following categories:

*Daily

*Weekly

*Monthly
*Quarterly
*Annually
*Dreams

Daily goals should be your monthly goals divided by your working days. So, if your monthly sales goal is $60,000 and you work 20 days this month, then your daily gross goal should be $3,000. Now, inside that daily goal, you should break down your most common items that you sell and create what a "great day" would look like. For instance, if you sold men's clothing, you could track the sales of suits, shirts, ties, socks, belts, sport jackets, slacks and jeans. Suits, in the example, make you the most gross, but not all of your customers come in for suits. Money can be made on all of these items, and like we have discussed already, a balanced approach to your sales will generally yield the largest results. A great day might mean selling 4 shirts, 4 ties, 16 socks, 2 belts, 1 sport jacket, 3 slacks and 3 pair of jeans. Get to know your product well enough to know what you need to sell each day to make the money you need to make.

Next, set weekly goals. Take your monthly goals and divide them by 4.2. This will take into account long and short months. All weekly goals should include EVERY common item you sell. If you go one week without selling a common item, there is only one reason for the failure. YOU DID NOT ASK FOR THE BUSINESS! That's right. I don't want to hear about how your customers did not have money or that it was some sort of bad luck or bad mojo. If you go a week without selling a common item, it is on you.

When we move to monthly goals, there are a couple of things that need to be factored. Consider seasonal ups and downs and inventory. Most business is seasonal, so know how the seasons affect your business and set goals accordingly. If there is a back-to-school rush on your product, then August should be huge and February pretty soft.

Also take inventory into account when setting your goals. If your sales are greatly affected by a new product launch, be ready to factor that into your work schedule and goal setting.

To take out some of these highs and lows, you may want to consider setting quarterly goals. While seasonal sales might still make your goal a little higher or lower, looking at your business quarterly will soften out five week months or months that end on a Thursday.

Next, look at your annual goals closely and make sure that your daily, weekly, and monthly goals add up to your annual goal. This is a common mistake. People will set their monthly goals at 100,000 per month, but make their annual goal 1 million. Do the math and set your goals where they align. Also while setting your annual goal, establish what growth is acceptable. For established large businesses 5-10% is normally a good goal. For emerging businesses, a 20% increase is outstanding and for small or new businesses, try projecting your third best month in the last year as your new baseline.

During your goal setting, it is okay to set some dreams. These do not necessarily need to fit into the above parameters, but they can. Huge savings accounts, job promotions, even saving for a family trip can all be "dreams". Write them down, too! The best way to get to Hawaii for Christmas is to say you want it and write it down. Ask yourself "What does it take to get there?" and "How can I start that journey TODAY?" Stephen Butler Leacock said, "It may be that those who do most, dream most."

DAY #20: GOAL SHEETS

"Our goals can only be reached through a vehicle of a plan, in which we must fervently believe, and upon which we must vigorously act. There is no other route to success." —Pablo Picasso

Creating an easy to use goal-tracking sheet is one of the first things that I try to establish with my customers. The idea is to take large goals and break them down into weekly and daily accomplishments. Just make sure that if you hit your little goals, that your big goal will be attained.

All goals need to work in harmony and must be established, tracked, and evaluated on an ongoing basis. First, let's take a look at the harmony of goals. You need to "get your thinking up". You cannot get accustomed to how much you sell from month-to-month and lose sight that more is attainable. Your goals must show that you can achieve greater heights and that you are motivated to set and reach larger goals. Remember, doing "better" is not a goal. You need to have a specific plan and track your success and failures.

An extremely useful tool when setting and tracking sales goals is "looking for zeros". Looking for zeros is a simple concept. When tracking your sales, try not to focus on what you are selling. Instead, focus on what you are NOT selling. The most effective way of reaching your goal is by making sure that you are selling at least SOME of everything and not just many of the items that you feel are the best or your favorite. A way to reinforce this mindset is to remind yourself of lessons you learned as a child in school.

For hundreds and hundreds of years, teachers have lectured their students on two concepts that, above all, will have the greatest effect on grades, learning, and success.

Concept number one: Come to school everyday, ready to learn.

Concept number two: Do not have any zeros.

You must instill these concepts into yourself. Work, just like school, is a grind, but going to work every day, prepared and ready for work, will give you the best shot at reaching their goals. Another useful aspect of your goal sheet is to think about, and log, the answers to these questions, at least, monthly:

*What is helping me become successful?

*What is stopping me?

*What do I need?

You should ask yourself each month, "What is helping me be successful?" When you get that answer, make sure you compliment those that are helping so they are aware that their actions are positively impacting others. I write about this in the "Compliments" chapter. Also, introspection like this can help you become the best version of yourself. Realizing that you are not alone on an island is comforting and useful for any service advisor.

Next, ask yourself, "What is stopping me?" Almost always, the answer is you! Remember, any time you point a finger at someone else, you have three more pointing back at you. But specifically, what got in your way this week or month? Do not let obstacles define you and does not let anyone get in your way of gaining the success you strive for. This question is tough for some and sometimes being honest with you is the toughest thing for any of us to do.

Finally, ask yourself, "What do I need?" This is particularly important if you have a supervisor or boss. Be specific with your needs and know the costs that are involved in your request. Look at things through their eyes but YOUR heart. Make them feel what you are feeling. If you do that, often you will get what you ask for!

FOURTH SATURDAY: NETWORKING

Maybe the most essential factor in whether or not you stay in the sales game long is networking. The broader footprint you have and the more people you come in contact with, the larger your circle of prospective customers becomes. Today, take a moment and focus on at least one aspect of networking.

*Know your current and future customers
*Get on the level of your customer
*Help people, first. Old and young
*Hone your elevator speech
*Social Media
*Set Goals
*Event hosting
*Business Cards

How well do you know your former, current, and future customers? Do you know where they work, attend church, or where their kids go to school? Can you describe your last contact with them? What was their determining factor in purchasing your product or service? If the answer is no, then you haven't been paying attention, but if the answer is yes, you need to start networking. Take, for example, knowing where your customers work. Have you offered others that work there your "Friends and Family" deal?

You could also take a photo with your customer and post it on your social media while tagging them. All of these are examples of knowing your current customers and mining your own customer database for new customers.

Once you get to know your customers, offer them help BEFORE you ask for their assistance. Offer assistance on projects that help the elderly or disadvantaged. Show your community that you are about more than business and they will send you more business.

It isn't a Quid Pro Quo situation; it is investing in your community. Sponsor a youth sports or youth group team or outing. Don't just give money, but give yourself to the cause. Help the youth group at the carwash or bake sale. Be a judge at an art fair and show people that you care about the kids. As usual, take pictures. Print a few with you and the kids and place it on your desk or on the wall of your workstation. You never know when a potential customer will recognize one of those kids. People want to work with folks that give back to the community. Be one of those people.

After you become involved, master your "elevator speech". An elevator speech, pitch, or statement is a short description of an idea, product, or company that explains the concept in a way such that any listener can understand it in a short period of time. The speech should last about 30 seconds, and it should be memorable.

Here is mine, "I am a corporate trainer for an oil company and my territory is Colorado to Memphis, Tennessee; South. My main customers are in the automotive industry and I essentially assist them by creating and implementing processes that help them sell everything better. Really, all I do is travel around and give speeches. I do have a clever hook though. I can teach anyone how to sell anything in two minutes!"

I love an elevator speech that makes a bold proclamation. First impressions are key and mastering your elevator speech is essential while networking. If you have 75 people at a function, time doesn't permit in depth discussions. You must tap into what makes YOU different than others. Remember your "ONE THING" from chapter one? It is that "ONE" word that must shine through during your elevator speech. My word is energy and when I give my 30-second overview, I am bringing THE ENERGY!!

Whatever your one word is, make that word shine through on social media. Have a very professional, but fun, LinkedIn profile and keep it stocked with current information. Facebook, Instagram and Twitter are huge. Have a space in each. Getting your own YouTube channel can be very powerful, as well and if you are selling specific goods, explore an Etsy store or Pinterest profile. Social media is here to stay and becoming a vibrant, unique user of it can greatly help your sales.

Next, a familiar theme in this book is to set networking goals.

Number of customers or prospective customers in your database, number of followers, percentage of email addresses captured and cell phone percentage captured are all good things to track and set goals for. Remember, you are 80% more likely to achieve your goal, IF YOU WRITE IT DOWN!

FOURTH SUNDAY: MOTIVATION AND INSPIRATION

On the last Sunday of the month, let's take it easy and read a few inspirational quotes.

"The quickest way to double your money is to fold it over and put it back in your pocket." – Will Rogers

"When I hear somebody sigh, 'Life is hard,' I am always tempted to ask, 'Compared to what?'"– Sydney Harris

"Do not let what you cannot do interfere with what you can do."– John Wooden

"Health is the greatest gift, contentment the greatest wealth, faithfulness the best relationship." – Buddha

"Everyone has inside of him a piece of good news. The good news is that you don't know how great you can be! How much you can love! What you can accomplish! And what your potential is! – Anne Frank

"Someone is sitting in the shade today because someone planted a tree a long time ago." – Warren Buffett

"No act of kindness, no matter how small, is ever wasted." – Aesop

"All you need is the plan, the road map, and the courage to press on to your destination." – Earl Nightingale

"One today is worth two tomorrows." – Ben Franklin

DAY #21: VOCABULARY

Three days left in your month. Are you where you need to be, or will the next two days be the difference in ballin' and getting balled out by the boss? How have the tips worked for you? Have you taken notes of your favorites or thought about the tips that fell flat? Today's tip is about improving your sales vocabulary. Each word you say to your customer matters. Have you analyzed yourself enough to know which words you currently use work best, or do you just "work each customer differently" aka, fly by the seat of your pants? In this chapter, we will explore some words that you should embrace and some others that you should avoid.

Word #1 to AVOID: Tell. You should never use the word "tell" with a customer. For example, "Let me tell you all about this new _____." Nobody likes to be told what to do. Telling people what to do or what to buy can quickly descend into an argument or negative feelings. Instead, I would like you to use the following word.

Word #1 to EMBRACE: Share: Instead of telling people something, I want you to share with everyone their options. For example, "Let me share with you the benefits of this _____." Sharing is a word that you should use scores of times each day.

"Let me share with you", "Please share with me, Mrs. Customer." Sharing gives people a sense of equality that is important during any sales negotiation. You do not want to present yourself in a condescending or know-it-all manner. Avoiding the use of the word "tell" and embracing the word "share" can help you accomplish the necessary tone during negotiations.

Word #2 to AVOID: Explain. One of the few words that evokes a more negative response than the word "tell" is "explain". NEVER explain things to your customer! EVER! For instance, "Mrs. Customer, let me explain to you what my manager or I mean." This is a terrible thing to say to any customer, but even worse if you are a salesman and you are "explaining" things to a female. Using this terminology, especially male to female, is often regarded as condescending or patronizing.

Word #2 to EMBRACE: "Discuss or Options" Instead of explaining yourself, try discussing the options or details. "Mrs. Customer, I would like to discuss the details about this matter." Or, "Mrs. Customer, I would to share a few options at hand." Always remember, everyone has options. Give your customers a few options that each has positive results. The customer can always think of negative options like not buying or waiting. It is your job to give them details and to discuss positive options.

Word #3 to AVOID: Cost/Price: Never share with your customers the cost or price of anything because both of those words likely have negative side effects. For instance, if I shared with you that I replaced my dishwasher and I felt that the appliance was "pricey", did we pay a little or a lot? A lot, right? If I share with you that my grandfather fought in a "costly" battle, did a few people die or a lot? A lot, right? Cost and price make people think of a lot. I don't want you to use words that make people that the amount they are paying is high. Instead, you should use the following word.

Word #3 to EMBRACE: Total Investment. Instead of sharing with the customer that the cost of your product is $400, share with them that the total investment of the product is $400. Few people are willing to "spend" a great deal, but many more are willing to "invest" in something. Something like WHATEVER YOU ARE SELLING!

DAY #22: WORD TRACKS.

Two evil words right there. WORD. TRACKS! I can hear them being repeated over and over in a deep, dark, scary, horror movie script. "WORD TRACKS" As I travel the country as a sales trainer the only thing that scares sales people more than word tracks is "ROLE PLAYING" BAHAHAHAHAHAHAHAHAHAHAHAHAHHH. Cue the foreboding music and shrill from the actors. In all seriousness, have you developed word tracks or a speech for every step in your sales process? Are you consistent from customer to customer and product to product? Are you still on the fence about whether or not using word tracks during sales is a good idea?

Allow me to answer that last question. YES! Many people, even those that do what I do, argue that word tracks are a bad idea and waste valuable time that could be used by being original. Word tracks often get a bad rap because they are too often confused with scripts. The difference between the two is massive and many professionals miss the nuance. First, word tracks SHOULD be original. I use word tracks and scripts during my training. I begin with an entire script and I go into each sentence with my trainees and I ask them to notate a word or two in each sentence that they like the best. Sentence by sentence we essentially edit the script into word tracks that are original to each trainee.

At the end of the session, I challenge them to immediately start using the words they chose. I remind the trainees that I do not want them to be robots, but I do want them to be consistent. When they become consistent with word tracks, they will become more confident and that confidence will lead to more sales.

Your word track expedition should begin with your meet and greet. Obviously you need to get, and use, the name of the customer right away. You will also need to give them your name, but how do you do this quickly? Have they been to your establishment before? Do they have an appointment? Each question is important. "Howdy! My name is Mitch, and yours is? Great, _____ are you here to see anyone in particular?"

I love asking if they are here to see anyone in particular. At many dealerships, service advisors are taught to ask if the customer has an appointment. This question inevitably leads to the "OK, you do? Do you know with whom?" I cut right to the point and ask if they are here to see anyone particular. If they are, I walk them to the person in question. If not, I get started selling. Another good by-product of this question is that it makes the customer feel that if they WERE here to see someone else, then you would assist in finding that person. This feeling helps lower the guard of the customer and makes you feel less "sales-y". This greeting subtly softens the customer and certainly pays dividends when used every day.

While there are word tracks that you can use throughout your sales process, I want to skip forward to the point after you have discussed your product or services, and begin the closing process. I love asking this question before I move in for the KILL! "Do you know?"

"Do you know what a brake fluid exchange does?" "Do you know what a four wheel alignment does?" "Do you know what replacing your spark plugs will do for you?" All of these questions have two answers: Yes or No. You need to be ready for either response. First, the most common response is "No". I have asked thousands of people, "Do you know what replacing your windshield wipers will do?" and I promise you, they STILL respond with "No". Now, with a small item like this, I normally make a joke like, "You don't know what replacing your wipers means?" and then we both laugh, but honestly, asking this question has been the key to success for many people I have met.

"Do you know what getting my service means?" I have found that 80% of the customers will respond with no and my response never, ever, changes. "What we are going to do is replace your current _____ with mine. It is going to help with _____ and it will help avoid _____."

Always start with the positive benefit your product or services brings and finish with a common negative item that purchasing your product or service helps avoid. Here are three examples labeled "A, B, and C" that illustrate how versatile "Do you know" is.

A. "Do you know what a brake fluid exchange does? Well, what we are going to do is remove all the old broken down fluid and replace it with brand new fluid. It is going to help you stop better and help those parts to last longer."

B. "Do you know what a spark plug replacement does? Well, what we are going to do is remove all the old broken down plugs and replace them with brand new plugs. It is going to help your engine run better and last longer."

C. "Do you know what a four wheel alignment does? Well, what we are going to do is make sure all four of your tires are running straight down the road. This is going to help your vehicle steer better and your tires to last longer."

Now, while most people will answer, "Do you know" with a "No", sometimes you get a customer that responds by saying "Yes".

When you get a yes, simply respond to the customer with "Great, then you know how important it is."

See, the logic here is, if the customer already sees the value in what you are offering, there is no need to go into details. Instead, you go for the close.

The close is your final word track to practice today. Every close in the world is the exact same so it is time you get to closing. A close has four elements:

1. Share with the customer what they need.
2. Share with the customer the total investment.
3. Share with the customer the time frame of closing.
4. All I need is your authorization.

Same close, every time. Watch.

A. "Do you know what a brake fluid exchange does? Well, what we are going to do is remove all the old broken down fluid and replace it with brand-new. It is going to help you stop better and those parts to last longer. That will bring your total investment to $145 and it will be completed by 3:00 pm. All I need is your authorization."

B. "Do you know what a spark plug replacement does? Well, what we are going to do is remove all the old broken down plugs and replace them with brand new plugs. It is going to help your engine run better and last longer. That will bring your total investment to $1106.54 and it will be completed by 3:00 pm. All I need is your authorization."

C. "Do you know what a four wheel alignment does? Well, what we are going to do is make sure all four of your tires are running straight down the road. This is going to help your vehicle steer better and your tires to last longer. That will bring your total investment to $145 and it will be completed by 3:00 pm. All I need is your authorization".

As you can see, the same close can be used for a brake fluid exchange, spark plug replacements and four-wheel alignments.

It all begins with asking, "Do you know what I am offering you?" and ends with "This is what you need. How much it is. When it will be ready and all I need is your authorization.

Never end your speech in a question, like, "How does that sound?" Or "What do you think?" All I need is your authorization is a much better word track. Practice, Practice, Practice because tomorrow is the most important day of the month.

LAST DAY: GO OUT AND SING IT!!!

OK, this is it. This is the last day of the month and the last tip that I will give you. But first, we need to talk about your choices. Remember, everyone has choices and you have to choose what you are going to do moving forward. The first choice is easy. You can finish this book and toss it in the trash. Forget everything you have read and put nothing new to practice. If you haven't been fired this month, chances are, you won't be fired next month. You can just continue doing what you have been doing and getting the same results you have been getting. That choice is easy.

Or, you can take ONE thing from this book and put it into practice. If it was I, and it once was, I would find that business card that you wrote your ONE word on the back of, and I would start showing EVERYONE the very best version of myself. Every co-worker you speak with or person at the drive-through window needs to see the best version of you on display. Be the most honest, trustworthy, hard working, knowledgeable person you can be, every minute of every day. Whatever your essence is, make sure each person that you come in contact with could guess your word.

My word is energy. Wherever I go, I am pretty sure I am going to be the most energetic person in the room. I may not be able to hang sheet rock, program a computer, or build a shelf, but what I can do is bring the energy. When I do have a bad day at work, and I don't have many, but when I do, it is normally because I coasted through the day and I didn't "bring it". I didn't bring the energy. When that is the case, I vow that the very next person I speak with, either a trainee in a class or the guy that is helping me at Home Depot, I will bring my energy. I will bring my effort.

Now, if you are willing to put to practice two things, today's tip is probably my second best tip of the month. Go out and SING IT!!! What I mean by that is, find your voice, your style and your tempo and then get out there and SING IT! From the word tracks we discussed, to the way you prospect, all of these processes are like lyrics to a song and a great performer can make any song great.

You have many performances within each day and you need to make each one of them count. Every time you interact with a customer, you should perform like that customer is one of two people. The first person you ever tried to sell to, or the last person you will ever have a chance to sell to. That sense of urgency will keep you and your performance sharp. Make every customer count and belt out for every person to hear, "I am a service advisor and I am proud of it!"